Wor

Purple Pinchers

and Other Hermit Crabs

Editor in Chief: Paul A. Kobasa
Supplementary Publications: Lisa Kwon, Christine Sullivan, Scott Thomas
Research: Mike Barr, Timothy J. Breslin, Cheryl Graham, Barbara Lightner, Loranne Shields
Graphics and Design: Kathy Creech, Sandra Dyrlund, Charlene Epple, Tom Evans
Permissions: Janet Peterson
Indexing: David Pofelski
Prepress and Manufacturing: Anne Dillon, Carma Fazio, Anne Fritzinger, Steven Hueppchen,
    Tina Ramirez
Writer: Sheri Reda

Our thanks to James Clark, aquarist at the Shedd Aquarium in Chicago, Illinois, for his help and advice.

For information about other World Book publications, visit our Web site at http://www.worldbook.com or call 1-800-WORLDBK (967-5325).

For information about sales to schools and libraries, call 1-800-975-3250 (United States); 1-800-837-5365 (Canada).

World Book, Inc.
233 N. Michigan Avenue
Chicago, IL 60601
U.S.A.

Library of Congress Cataloging-in-Publication Data
Purple pinchers and other hermit crabs.
    p. cm. -- (World Book's animals of the world)
  Summary: "An introduction to purple pinchers and other hermit crabs,
presented in a highly illustrated, question and answer format.
Features include fun facts, glossary, resource list, index, and
scientific classification list"--Provided by publisher.
  Includes bibliographical references and index.
  ISBN-13: 978-0-7166-1333-6
  ISBN-10: 0-7166-1333-6
  1. Hermit crabs--Juvenile literature. 2. Coenobita clypeatus—
Juvenile literature. I. World Book, Inc. II. Series.
QL444.M33P87 2007
595.3'87--dc22
                    2006013233

Printed in Malaysia
1 2 3 4 5 6 7 8 09 08 07 06

Picture Acknowledgements: Cover: © Fred Bavendam, Minden Pictures; © Georgette Douwma, Taxi/Getty Images; © Dwight Kuhn; © Krystyna Szulecka, Alamy Images; © Frank Yuwono, ShutterStock.

© Fred Bavendam, Minden Pictures 57; © Paul Cowan, ShutterStock 49; © Georgette Douwma, Taxi/Getty Images 51; © Christian Gillett, Animals Animals 55; © Frank Greenaway, Dorling Kindersley/Getty Images 9; © Stacy Griffith 35, 37; © Dwight Kuhn 3, 4, 5, 13, 15, 17, 19, 23, 25, 27, 29, 31, 39, 41, 59, 61; © Vanessa Pike-Russell, Crab Street Journal 5, 53; © Plowes ProteaPix 33; © Krystyna Szulecka, Alamy Images 45; © Frank Yuwono, ShutterStock 43, 47.

Illustrations: WORLD BOOK illustration by John Fleck 8; WORLD BOOK illustration by Paul Perreault 21.

World Book's Animals of the World

Purple Pinchers
and Other Hermit Crabs

World Book, Inc.
a Scott Fetzer company
Chicago

Contents

What Is a Hermit Crab?

A hermit crab is a special kind of crab. All crabs belong to a group of animals called arthropods *(AHR thruh podz)*. Arthropods have jointed legs and bodies that are divided into segments, or pieces. An arthropod is an invertebrate—an animal that has no backbone inside its body. Most arthropods, however, do have a skeleton. But it is on the outside, not the inside, of their body. An arthropod's outer skeleton is a hard, shell-like object called an exoskeleton *(EHK soh SKEHL uh tuhn)*. Hermit crabs have an exoskeleton on only part of their body. They have no exoskeleton on their abdomen.

Hermit crabs live in shells that other animals formed and then left behind. A hermit crab hangs onto its shell with its back legs and drags the shell around with it. When a hermit crab grows larger, it looks for a bigger shell in which to live.

Most hermit crabs are marine animals, meaning they live their entire lives in the ocean. Purple pinchers, however, are land-dwelling hermit crabs. They are born in the ocean, but live most of their lives on dry land.

A purple pincher

7

What Is in That Shell?

A hermit crab has two pairs of antennae and round eyes on the ends of eyestalks.

Hermit crabs have 10 legs, but only 6 legs show. These front 6 legs are known as walking legs. Hermit crabs keep their 4 back legs inside their shell. The back legs are much smaller than the walking legs.

The front pair of legs ends in claws, or pinchers. The left front leg has a large pincher, which the crab uses for moving around and defending itself. When the animal is hiding inside its shell, it uses this pincher to seal off the shell's opening. The right front leg has a smaller pincher, which the crab uses to eat and drink. Both front pinchers have thick layers of exoskeleton.

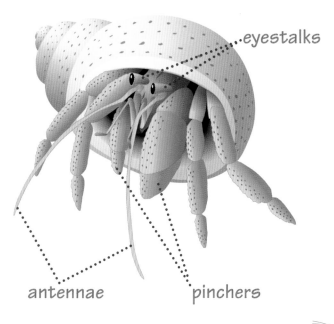

eyestalks

antennae   *pinchers*

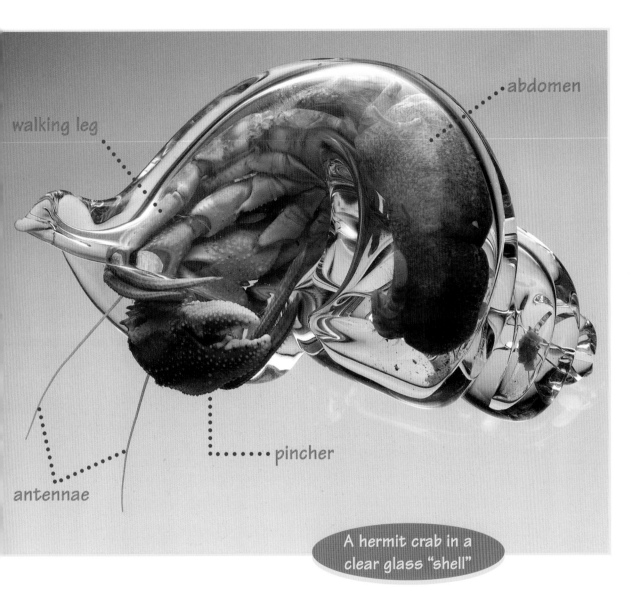

walking leg

abdomen

antennae

pincher

A hermit crab in a
clear glass "shell"

Where Do Purple Pinchers Live in the Wild?

Land-dwelling hermit crabs live in many parts of the world where climates are tropical. These tropical regions have, for the most part, warm temperatures year around and plentiful rainfall. Of the many kinds of land-dwelling hermit crabs, only purple pinchers live in the United States. They are found in southern Florida.

Purple pinchers also live on Caribbean islands and in other tropical habitats as far south as Venezuela. In fact, purple pinchers are often called Caribbeans.

Purple pinchers sometimes live a distance away from the water. No matter where they live in the wild, however, purple pinchers always migrate back to the seashore so that their eggs can be hatched in the ocean.

World Map

Arctic Ocean

North America

Europe

Asia

Atlantic Ocean

Pacific Ocean

Africa

Equator

South America

Indian Ocean

Pacific Ocean

Australia

Southern Ocean

Antarctica

Map Key

Where purple pinchers live

N

W

E

S

11

How Big
Do Purple
Pinchers Get?

Purple pinchers begin life as the tiniest of creatures that float on the surface of the sea. It is a good thing that a female hermit crab lays a lot of eggs, because whales and other big sea creatures gobble up most of the young crabs!

The purple pinchers that manage to survive soon grow much bigger. A smallish purple pincher bought for a pet might be less than 1 inch (2.5 centimeters) long. A large purple pincher could be more than 3 inches (7.6 centimeters) long.

Purple pinchers of
different sizes

13

What Kind of Personality Might a Purple Pincher Have?

Hermits are people who live by themselves. They often stay indoors, and they usually avoid others. A hermit crab lives all its life inside a shell. It never leaves its shell except when it moves into another shell.

Purple pinchers are a kind of hermit crab. But unlike people who are hermits, purple pinchers like company. In the wild, they live in groups and are fairly social.

Most purple pinchers are friendly. But, just like people, each purple pincher is unique. Some purple pinchers are shy, while others are bold. There are purple pinchers that like to play a lot, while others are less active. Some purple pinchers enjoy being handled, others may want to be left alone.

Most purple pinchers get along well with other purple pinchers. Sometimes they fight over shells, but it is rare for purple pinchers to be aggressive with another hermit crab.

14

A purple pincher peers from under a leaf

What Should You Look for When Choosing a Purple Pincher ?

Purple pinchers are inexpensive and cute, and they like to play. These crabs are fun to watch and easy to care for.

When you buy a purple pincher, it is important to make sure you get a healthy animal. Go to a pet shop where the staff have a lot of experience in caring for hermit crabs. Look for an active hermit crab that you find interesting.

Purple pinchers are relatively safe pets. Some types of pets—certain turtles or aquarium fish, for instance—can carry diseases that may be caught by humans and that can make humans very ill. Hermit crabs do not usually carry any such diseases.

An active purple pincher

What Does a Purple Pincher Eat and Drink?

Purple pinchers are omnivores—meaning they eat everything—fruit, plants, fish, and even red meat. It is best to feed crabs hermit-crab food and a variety of human foods. Crabs especially like fruit and cuttlefish. To keep life interesting for your pets, offer them a balanced diet, but vary that diet.

Purple pinchers are very sensitive to pesticides (bug-killing chemicals). Make sure you feed your purple pincher food grown without pesticides or else rinse the food very well.

Purple pinchers drink mostly fresh water. But sometimes they like to drink salt water, so offer both kinds of water. Do not make salt water for your pet from ordinary table salt, which contains a chemical called iodine. Iodine is harmful to hermit crabs. Use salt from a pet store that is made for fish aquariums.

Finally, chlorine—a chemical put in tap water to kill germs—can also kill hermit crabs. Give your crab purified, bottled water instead of tap water.

A purple pincher feeding

Where Should a Pet Purple Pincher Be Kept?

Purple pinchers are not demanding creatures, but they need a particular kind of warm, humid habitat, or living place, or they cannot survive.

To give your purple pincher a good habitat, purchase a glass or plastic aquarium tank. Make sure the tank has a secure lid so your hermit crab does not climb out. Also, make sure the lid can be opened to allow air to flow into the tank when needed.

Keep a thermometer in the tank. Knowing the temperature allows you to make adjustments to keep the inside of the tank between 75 and 85 °F (24 and 29 °C). Use a low-wattage, incandescent light bulb to keep the tank warm, or buy an under-tank heater to warm the tank from below.

It is a good idea to keep a hygrometer in the tank to measure humidity, that is, the amount of water vapor in the air. Hermit crabs need an environment of around 70 percent humidity. You can use sea sponges soaked in water to maintain the humidity in a tank.

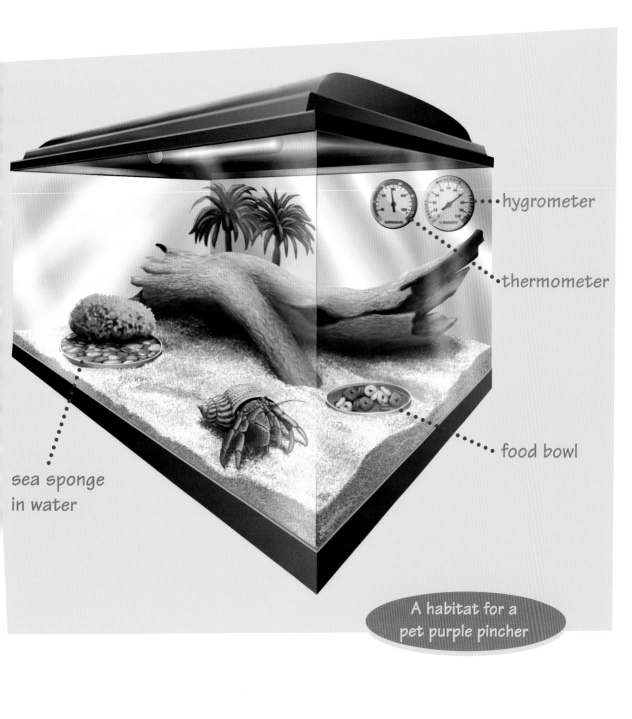

hygrometer

thermometer

food bowl

sea sponge
in water

A habitat for a
pet purple pincher

How Does a Habitat Become a Crabitat?

With attention to a few details, you can turn a good habitat, or living place, into a great crabitat! Purple pinchers like to dig and to bury themselves, so they need bedding twice as deep as they are tall. Finely crushed coral from a pet store is ideal. Play sand or beach sand also makes good bedding, and sand is easy to replace when you clean the tank each month. For variety, you can put coconut fiber or fine gravel in part of the tank.

Put two shallow bowls in the tank: one for fresh water and one for food. Do not use metal bowls, because metal can be harmful to hermit crabs. If your crabs are small, put a sponge in the water bowl so the crabs will not get trapped in the water and drown. Some crabs need a third bowl for saltwater.

Add cork bark or driftwood to the tank so your crabs can exercise and play. Add hollow logs, dig your crab some small caves, and put in some plants so your hermit crab can hide when it wants to be alone. And don't forget shells. Supply a variety of shells for your purple pinchers to grow into.

Items in a crabitat

How Do You Care for a Crabitat?

Purple pinchers have things they need done to their crabitat on a daily, weekly, and monthly basis.

Daily—Take uneaten food out of the tank and add new food. Change the water. Also, check the temperature and humidity of the tank. If the humidity is too high, open the top of the tank a bit. If the humidity is too low, add an extra sponge to the water bowl.

Weekly—Replace the dry food and water and scoop out the crab's droppings. Don't forget to clean or replace the sponge. To clean a sponge for reuse, first rinse it, let it dry completely, then microwave it for about 2 minutes.

Monthly—Wipe the tank and wash everything in it, but never use soap or cleaning chemicals. You can also microwave the pieces of driftwood and cork in the tank for about 2 minutes to clean them. (Ask a grown-up for help with the microwave.) Replace the tank's bedding each month.

A crabitat

How Do You Bathe a Purple Pincher?

Purple pinchers keep themselves clean. Although they do not need to be bathed, purple pinchers can benefit from a bath every week or two. This helps the animals flush out their shells and wet their gills.

There are two ways to bathe a purple pincher. One way is to fill a small bowl with about ¼ inch (0.64 cm) of warm, chlorine-free water. Gently place the purple pincher upside down in the small bowl. The animal will turn over and walk around, shaking out any debris within its shell. The other way is to fill a small bowl with warm, chlorine-free water and gently dunk the purple pincher in the water two or three times. Do not put the crab under the water for too long or it will drown! After the bath, let the purple pincher walk around in a clean box lined with a paper towel.

In addition to bathing, many owners also use spray bottles to mist their purple pincher. This helps the animal to stay moist. Hermit crabs usually become more active after mistings.

A purple pincher
having a bath

27

How Does a
Purple Pincher Play?

Purple pinchers are nocturnal creatures, which means they are more active at night than during the day.

To encourage your pets to be as active as possible when they are awake, add toys to their tank. Purple pinchers love to play. In addition to providing cork and coral, you can add many other playthings. For example, hermit crabs like to run around plants and hide in caves.

Purple pinchers like to climb, too. They will climb over rocks, driftwood, and unpainted clay flowerpots. Just make sure they cannot use their toys to get high enough to climb out of their tank.

If you supervise your purple pinchers so they do not get lost, you can let them outside the tank to explore. If your house is warm, you can even put your crabs, one at a time, into a plastic "hamster ball" and let them roll around a room.

A purple pincher
climbs over a pot

29

How Can You Coax a Purple Pincher to Walk on Your Hand?

Purple pinchers vary in their reactions to being handled. While some like to be handled, others do not. When handling your purple pincher, never try to take it out of its shell. Most hermit crabs will risk injury to avoid being pulled from their shell.

When handling your purple pincher, let it get to know you. Pick it up gently by the back of its shell. Make sure you do not create any big shadows or make any sudden movements that would scare your purple pincher. Simply hold your hand out and place the crab on your flat, outstretched palm. Be patient; it may take a while for your crab to feel safe.

If your purple pincher pinches you, do not try to pull it off. It will only pinch harder. To get a hermit crab to release its hold, put the crab under warm, running water. If that doesn't cause the crab to release its hold, dunk the animal gently in a bowl of lukewarm water.

A purple pincher on an
outstretched hand

How Do Purple Pinchers Breed in the Wild?

Pet purple pinchers do not have young, because their eggs will not hatch in a tank. In the wild, however, hermit crabs spend a lot of time getting ready to have their young.

At mating time, some kinds of hermit crabs get together in large groups, called "crab conventions." At conventions, crabs seek out new and larger shells and find mates.

After mating, a female crab carries her eggs on the left side of her abdomen until they are ready to hatch. Then she scurries to the ocean and releases the eggs.

The young of purple pinchers are extremely tiny. They spend the beginning of their lives as plankton, or small water organisms floating on the surface of the ocean. Fish and other sea creatures eat most of them.

If a purple pincher escapes being eaten, it eventually comes ashore to begin its life as a land hermit crab.

A convention of
hermit crabs

Why Does a Crab Bury Itself?

Like most hermit crabs, purple pinchers molt, or shed, their exoskeleton and grow a strong, fresh one to cover everything but their abdomen. Most hermit crabs molt at least once every 18 months. Young hermit crabs molt more often.

Molting allows purple pinchers to grow, but the process also poses problems. While they are molting, the crabs are weak. Their sensitive skin is uncovered, so the crab can dry out or be easy prey for other animals. For these reasons, crabs usually bury themselves while they are molting. Leave your purple pincher alone if you think it is molting. You only need to investigate if you smell a strong fishy smell, which can indicate a dead crab.

In time your crab will reappear with a fresh, new exoskeleton. Be sure to have larger shells available, as your crab will most likely need a new one after molting. Most hermit crabs gain bulk as their exoskeletons swell and harden.

A hermit crab buried in a sand tunnel during its molting period

35

How Can You Tell When a Hermit Crab Is About to Molt?

Some hermit crabs give no sign that they are ready to molt. But others may look different and act strange. Here are some of the signs of molting you might notice in a hermit crab:

- Its eyes may get cloudy.

- It may eat and drink more than usual and grow a sac of fat. Then, it may stop eating and become less active.

- It may dig a lot.

If your hermit crab shows several of these signs, place it in a warm, humid tank by itself. Supply food and water dishes and 6 inches (15 centimeters) of such bedding as moist sand. If your crab is molting above ground, spray it lightly with mist. Otherwise, leave it alone.

After it has molted and grown a new exoskeleton, it will reemerge. Let your crab eat its old exoskeleton for the nutrition it provides.

An empty exoskeleton
molted by a hermit crab

What Kinds of Shells Do Hermit Crabs Like?

All land hermit crabs need new shells to fit them as they grow. For that reason, you should supply your hermit crab with many shells in various sizes.

Different hermit crabs like different kinds of shells, and they also enjoy "shopping" for shells. Hermit crabs will spend a lot of time checking out new shells, so replace them from time to time.

Purple pinchers like roundish shells with circular openings, smooth insides, and a coil leading off to the right. They usually prefer short coils so they do not have too much shell to drag around. Pet purple pinchers have no preference between unpainted, natural shells and decorated shells.

Different kinds of hermit crabs prefer other kinds of shells. Ecuadorians (see page 44), for example, like shells with wide, oval openings. Be sure to choose your shells carefully so your crabs will be happy with the selection.

A purple pincher
examining shells

What Is That Chirping Sound?

Hermit crabs, including purple pinchers, sometimes make a chirping sound, but no one has quite figured out how they make this sound. Scientists have suggested that a hermit crab makes these sounds by rubbing its legs against one another.

However this noise is made, a hermit crab can sometimes be heard to produce it when it is annoyed. For example, when another hermit crab is climbing on it or when it is engaged in the occasional shell fight.

Hermit crabs have other ways of making noises than chirping. Sometimes an animal may make clicking sounds by tapping on its shell with its claw. At other times, a hermit crab may bang its shell against the shell of another crab to produce a noise.

Hermit crabs usually make more noise at night, when they are more active.

Purple pinchers use their shells to make noise

Who Has the Biggest Purple Pincher of All?

Purple pinchers are not the only hermit crabs with a purple pincher. Indonesian crabs have much larger pinchers that are also purple.

Some Indonesian crabs use a coconut for a home, instead of a shell. Other Indonesian crabs prefer to live in a turbo shell (a shell once belonging to a kind of snail called a turbo).

Crabs that live inland from the sea, such as the Indonesian, usually find their first shell on the shore, since they are born in the ocean. Then these crabs move inland. But, hermit crabs go to the ocean periodically to allow the female to lay her eggs in the sea. The males accompany the females on this trip. Traveling back to the ocean gives such hermit crabs as the Indonesian an opportunity to find new shells on the shore. Land hermit crabs can also sometimes find new shells inland that have been abandoned by other hermit crabs.

An Indonesian
hermit crab

Who Needs Extra Care?

One type of hermit crab, the Ecuadorian from South America, needs more care than many other hermit crabs.

Ecuadorians are especially sensitive to changes in temperature and humidity. To keep a more constant temperature and humidity level in the animal's habitat, owners usually provide deeper bedding for their Ecuadorian than would be provided for a purple pincher. Ecuadorians also need salt water in their habitat for drinking and bathing.

These crabs also are fussy about their shells. The body of an Ecuadorian is wider and flatter than that of the Caribbean crabs, so Ecuadorians prefer bigger shell openings. If you do not provide an Ecuadorian with its preferred shell, it may refuse to switch shells, even when its current shell becomes much too small.

An Ecuadorian crab

Who Is Called a Rug?

Tawny hermit crabs are often called rugs. This nickname comes from their scientific name (see page 65), which is *Coenobita rugosus.*

Some rugs are brown with weak purplish highlights. Other rugs are whitish with gray highlights. Many rugs have fine stripes across the top of the large claw.

Rugs are seldom available as pets. They are found in the wild from the East African coast on the Indian Ocean to regions of the southwestern Pacific.

A rug, or
Coenobita rugosus

Who Has Red Antennae?

Concave hermit crabs, or cavs, look a lot like Ecuadorian and Indonesian crabs. But the cavs' bright red antennae set them apart. Also, unlike other crabs, the cav has a slight curve to the underside of its eyestalks. The eyes of a cav can be red or black and are very large, compared with other hermit crabs.

Cavs get their nickname from their scientific name (see page 65), which is *Coenobita cavipes*. These crabs enjoy digging and they sometimes like to remain buried for long periods. They especially enjoy and need salt water.

Cavs are not often available in pet stores. In the wild, cavs are found from East Africa to the western Pacific.

Three cavs, or
Coenobita cavipes

Who Needs Carrots on the Menu?

Red strawberry crabs need a lot of carotene to maintain their color. Carotene is an orange-red pigment found in many foods. Carrots are a good source of carotene. So, strawberry crabs need to eat their carrots to keep their color from fading.

Strawberry crabs are probably the easiest land hermit crabs to recognize. Most strawberry crabs are bright red.

In the wild, strawberry crabs live near the shorelines of the Indian and Pacific oceans. Many are found in Australia. In order to keep the number of strawberry crabs from declining in the wild, however, the government of Australia does not allow strawberry crabs to be captured and sold as pets. Pet dealers can still obtain these crabs from other countries.

Strawberry crabs

Who Is a "Garbage Disposal"?

Australian crazy crabs, or Aussies, are especially active scavengers that feed on decaying things. In the wild, Aussies come out at night and eat up dead fish. They also eat seaweed and fruits that may wash up on the beach. If a pet Aussie gets out of its tank, it may head straight for the garbage can.

In Australia, these crabs live together in large colonies. Because this species is not endangered, Aussies are readily available in pet stores.

Crazy crabs range in color from cream to red or light brown. They have dark markings on their bodies and flattened eyestalks.

An Aussie

Who Is the World's Largest Land Crab?

Most hermit crabs are small, but the coconut crab is not like most crabs! This land crab, which lives on islands in the western Pacific and Indian oceans, can grow to about 3 feet (0.9 meters) from claw to claw. An adult coconut crab can weigh as much as 9 pounds (4 kilograms).

Of course, it can be hard to find a shell big enough to fit a coconut crab, but that does not bother this animal. After it outgrows the largest shell it can find, a coconut crab goes through a metamorphosis, or change. Unlike other hermit crabs, the coconut crab grows a shell of its own. This shell forms when the coconut crab is about a year old.

Coconut crabs breathe through modified gills, but cannot breathe in the water. They burrow in limestone, coral rock, or in undergrowth on land. Still, coconut crabs need to lay their eggs in water, and they need water to keep their gills wet.

A coconut crab
climbing a tree

55

How Do Some Hermit Crabs Decorate Their Shells?

Land hermit crabs are picky about their shells. They seem to "shop" for the perfect shell. Once they find one they like, they move in and simply enjoy it.

Cousins of land hermit crabs include more than 800 kinds of marine hermit crabs. At least one kind—the *Dardanus* crab—moves into a shell and then decorates it.

Dardanus crabs often place sea anemones on their shells, which works well for both animals. The hermit crab gets a little extra protection from other sea creatures, because sea anemones are poisonous, which makes other creatures wary of them. The anemones get leftover food from the crab and a free ride.

A *Dardanus* crab with sea anemones on its shell

How Can You Be Sure Your Purple Pincher Is Healthy?

Purple pinchers that are ill are usually sluggish and do not move their antennae around. (Purple pinchers that are getting ready to molt may act this way, too.) Check that the crabitat has the correct temperature and humidity (see page 20).

The number-one killer of pet hermit crabs is the lack of a proper habitat. Hermit crabs must have a warm, moist environment. If they get too hot or dry, they will die. Be sure to keep your crabitat away from windows and other sunny spots. Never leave your hermit crab in a car where it can become overheated.

Sometimes, purple pinchers can get a fungus. To get rid of this fungus, bathe your crab in a saltwater and then a freshwater bath. Small parasites that feed on crabs can sometimes invade a tank. To get rid of them, bathe your hermit crab. Then, clean its tank with a solution of vinegar and water and rinse it with chlorine-free water. Finally, replace the tank bedding and clean everything else that was in the tank. If the parasites remain, call a veterinarian for additional advice.

A purple pincher

What Are Your Responsibilities as an Owner?

Hermit crabs are not very demanding pets, but like most unusual pets, they do require some special care. Make sure you do your research and get to know all you can about hermit crabs before you buy one. Do not buy a hermit crab if you think you will get tired of it.

If you do decide to adopt a pet hermit crab, make sure you choose a healthy one. It can be very hard to nurse a sick hermit crab back to health, and even an experienced crab owner might find that difficult.

Avoid buying the most exotic of hermit crabs. Some of them do not survive well as pets. Instead, choose crabs that can be happy with tank life.

A purple pincher

Hermit Crab Fun Facts

→ Groups of hermit crabs sometimes team up so that one crab can climb out of the tank. One crab climbs on top of another, making a stack of crabs that reaches to the top of the tank. The crab at the top of the stack will climb out and explore.

→ If hermit crabs get too warm, they will fight to get into smaller, lighter shells. Each hermit crab will force the next smaller crab out of its shell, and the smallest crab will be left with no shell.

→ Rough handling, a move to a new tank, or even a difficult molt can cause a hermit crab to drop limbs (legs). In order to grow new limbs, the crab will need to molt again.

→ Only when hermit crabs are out of their shell can you tell males apart from females. Females have tiny openings called gonopores on their third legs. Males have a tube.

→ Coconut crabs eat coconuts. The crabs pry them open with their claws in order to eat the coconut meat inside.

62

Glossary

antennae Long, delicate sense organs on the heads of almost all insects and most other arthropods.

arthropod A member of a large group of animals that includes insects and crustaceans; arthropods have jointed legs and hard outer skeletons, called exoskeletons.

exoskeleton The hard outer shell that covers and protects the bodies of arthropods.

eyestalk The stalk that holds the eye of crabs, lobsters, and shrimps.

gill A feathery, blood-filled organ that some animals use to take in oxygen from the surrounding water. When land hermit crabs are first hatched, they live in water and breathe using gills.

gonopore The reproductive opening of the female hermit crab.

habitat The area where an animal lives, which contains everything the animal needs to survive.

hygrometer An instrument used to measure the amount of humidity, or water vapor, in the air.

invertebrate An animal that does not have a backbone.

marine An animal or plant that is of or found in the ocean.

molt To shed old shell, skin, feathers, or other body coverings.

nocturnal An animal that is active in the night.

omnivore An animal that eats both animals and plants.

parasite An organism (living creature) that feeds on and lives on or in the body of another organism, often causing harm to the being on which it feeds.

pesticide A chemical that is used to kill harmful insects.

scavenger An animal that feeds on decaying things. Vultures, jackals, some snails and beetles, and crabs are examples of scavengers.

tropical An animal or plant that lives in (or comes from) regions near Earth's equator. These regions have mostly warm temperatures the year around and plentiful rainfall.

Index

(**Boldface** indicates a photo, map, or illustration.)

For more information about Purple Pinchers and Other Hermit Crabs, try these resources:

Hermit Crabs: Complete Pet Owner's Manual, by
   Sue Fox, Barron's Educational Series, 2000

Land Hermit Crabs, by Philippe De Vosjoli,
   BowTie Press, 2nd edition, 2005

Quick and Easy Hermit Crab Care,
   TFH Publications, 2003

http://crabstreetjournal.com/
http://www.hermitcrabsassociation.com/phpBB/
   index.php
http://www.hermit-crabs.com/species.html

Hermit Crab Classification

Scientists classify animals by placing them into groups. The animal kingdom is a group that contains all the world's animals. Phylum, class, order, and family are smaller groups. Each phylum contains many classes. A class contains orders, an order contains families, and a family contains genuses. One or more species belong to each genus. Here is how the animals in this book fit into this system.

Animals with jointed legs and their relatives (Phylum Arthropoda)
Crustaceans (Subphylum Crustacea)
Crabs and their relatives (Class Malacostraca)
Decapods (Order Decapoda)

Hermit crabs and their relatives (Superfamily Paguroidea)

Land-dwelling hermit crabs (Family Coenobitidae)

Purple pincher, or Caribbean hermit crab .... *Coenobita clypeatus*

Coconut hermit crab .... *Coenobita birgus latro*
Indonesian hermit crab .... *Coenobita brevimanus*
Concave land hermit crab .... *Coenobita cavipes*
Ecuadorian hermit crab .... *Coenobita compressus*
Strawberry land hermit crab .... *Coenobita perlatus*
Tawny hermit crab .... *Coenobita rugosus*
Australian crazy hermit crab .... *Coenobita variabilis*

Marine-dwelling hermit crabs (Family Diogenidae)

Various genera of hermit crabs, including several species of *Dardanus* crabs, belong to the family Diogenidae.